You

A BEGINNER'S GUIDE TO BUILDING A YOUTUBE CHANNEL AUDIENCE AND MAKE PASSIVE INCOME

BOOK DESCRIPTION

YouTube is the leading online Video hosting platform and the second most popular search engine after Google. YouTube's parent company is Google. Thus, leveraging both YouTube and Google can give you an upper hand in accessing and directing traffic to your video. With over a billion viewers and almost a million unique visits a day, YouTube is such a gigantic exposure that any serious video creator can simply not ignore.

This guide is geared towards enabling you take advantage of this immense potential by showing you how to create your own YouTube Channel, build a massive audience and maximize on passive income.

It starts with a beginner's approach by proving to you why you ought to be on YouTube and unveiling to you immense benefits that you can derive from having a YouTube channel. It goes further by practically walking you through step-by-step instructions to building your own passive income-generating YouTube channel.

Making good quality Youtube videos is a must if indeed you have to tap into multi-million dollar potential offered by Youtube. This guide introduces you to items you need as a starter to shoot your video and advance on that as you grow to become a professional Youtube video creator.

Should you find your video shooting skills wanting or not having enough time to manage your Channel, this guide provides you with great alternatives that can enable you get the required people to help you create and run your Youtube Channel.

Making money is obviously a great endeavor for any videopreneur (video entrepreneur). You too can make money. Indeed, you ought to do it in order to recoup your cost and investment and earn some profit on top. The purpose of this guide is to help you get rich through your videopreneurship endeavors. We walk you through ways to make money off your Youtube channel, how to raise funds the easiest way possible and how to drive traffic to your channel and blog. We also show you how to share your knowledge via tutorials through your Youtube channel.

Last but not least, like any other shrewd entrepreneur, you need to scale-up your earnings. This guide provides you with hands-on practical information on how you can grow your channel to achieve multiple passive income streams while taking advantage of automation.

Enjoy reading!

ABOUT THE AUTHOR

George Pain is an entrepreneur, author and business consultant. He specializes in setting up online businesses from scratch, investment income strategies and global mobility solutions. He has built several businesses from the ground up, and is excited to share his knowledge with readers. Here is a list of his books.

Books of George Pain

DISCLAIMER

CONTENTS

INTRODUCTION

Studies have shown that most content readers are twice as likely view video content than read text content. It also shows that people are thrice as likely to remember what they have viewed than what they read. It further shows that videos are the de facto way of accessing content online by the millennial generation. This simply means that video content is the online king of the future. You need not be left off this trend.

Videopreneurship has become one of the most lucrative ventures online. Leveraging your Youtube Channel with your blog and other ventures such as affiliate marketing and ecommerce can have a multiplier effect to your online business. This guide is geared towards empowering you to take advantage of these facts to build an audience and propel both your active and passive income.

Becoming a multimillion-dollar online entrepreneur is the dream of many. Yet, you cannot achieve this by laboring like a donkey for the sake of working for money. You need to offload your work by letting money work for you. Automation is the key to working smart. In this guide, you will learn ways to automate your

YouTube channel income so that you can not only make money off your channel but grow your channel to earn big-figure passive income while you increasingly sweat less and less.

Keep reading!

SHOULD YOU CREATE A YOUTUBE CHANNEL?

YouTube is no doubt the leading Video hosting company in the world. It is also the second largest search engine after Google. The two factors combined make YouTube an inevitable choice to build an audience and monetize your videos.

Why YouTube?

They say that figures don't lie. The following are inspiring facts that point to why you already ought to present in the YouTube ecosystem;

- YouTube has over 1.3 Billion people who use it to view videos - This means that you have an over one-billion-people potential market for your video and products. This is such a huge market that you cannot find anywhere else.
- YouTube gets 4,300 hours of video upload every minute - This is an indicator of the reputation that YouTube has in terms of the volume of video content creators. You are not alone in this endeavor.

- Over 4.9 million videos are viewed on YouTube every day – This shows you the potential views per day for your video.

- YouTube gets over 900,000 unique visits each and every day - Unique visitors are an indicator of the new potential that unveils everyday on YouTube.

- Each month, YouTube receives a total 3.25 billion hours of views – Just getting 1% of these billions of hours in a month is a startling endeavor. Yet, you have a potential not just for 1% but much more%! This is a whole new world for you.

- Over 70% of YouTube viewers are outside the United States – YouTube is a global phenomenon. Unlike so many other services on internet that have US-based massive following, YouTube is well distributed globally. This means that you are not geographically constrained in terms of targeting. The globe is truly your village.

- Mobile views per day have hit the 1 million mark – It is no doubt that the internet landscape is gradually shifting away from desktop towards mobile. This is potential that continues to grow. The great advantage of YouTube, unlike other web content, it is not such constrained by screen dimensions. Thus, you don't have to bother as to whether your YouTube video is mobile-friendly or not. It is already configured to be so by default.

- There are currently over 10,000 videos that have garnered over 1 billion views – Getting 1 billion views is no mean achievement. In terms of monetization, this is hundreds of millions of dollars. You have potential to achieve this. If others have achieved it, why not you?

- The average number of minutes spent on mobile views per session is 40 minutes – This gives you a hint of the expected length of your video. With internet costs continuing to decline, there is a general rise in in the average number of minutes spent on YouTube mobile video views. This will continue on upward trends as more people shift to smartphone usage over time.

What is a YouTube Channel?

A YouTube Channel is a user's profile page that appears when one registers as a YouTube member. The following are specific details that appear on one's YouTube Channel;

1. Account name – This is basically your name (personal account) or the name of your organization (business account)

2. Account type – This is the nature of your account. It is either personal account or business account.

3. A personal description – This is a brief description of your profile.
4. Videos one uploads for public view (public videos) – These are videos that you upload to be shared with members.
5. List of members who are friends – These are people whom you have accepted their friend's request and thus follow your YouTube Channel.

YouTube Account Types

There are basically two types of YouTube Accounts;

- YouTube personal channel
- YouTube business channel

What is YouTube Personal Account?

YouTube personal account is an account opened and setup by YouTube to be used by a single individual. Thus, you can only log in using your personal Gmail account.

See the next section for details on how to open a Personal Account.

What is YouTube Business Account?

YouTube business account is an account opened with a different name (business name) that is separate from your personal name. Thus, other persons are allowed to log in and manage the account. You can have an administrator and even assistants to help you manage your channel.

See the next section for details on how to open a YouTube Business Account.

Why create a YouTube Channel?

There are several reasons as to why one would want to create a YouTube Channel. Each person has his/her own reasons. However the following are the common reasons;

1. To upload and share personal videos with others – If you have a personal video, probably about your birthday party, your graduation ceremony, your wedding anniversary, etc, you can share it with your friends.
2. To offer tutorials – Video tutorials are increasingly becoming common. You can create "How-To" video tutorials on any topic that you have good knowledge, skills and experience in.
3. To share talents – You can share your talents with others such as cooking, knitting, programming, crafting, etc.
4. To promote products – Marketers are increasingly using YouTube videos as a way to launch product demos,

introduce new product features and persuade potential customers to buy their products.

5. To evaluate a video before launching it – Artists often pre-launch videos of their movies or songs so that their fans can evaluate it. This enables the artists to fine-tune them before final launch. This is a great way of gathering fans' opinions and their responses about areas that need improvement.

6. To make money – Making money online has transitioned into a full-time career for many. However, whether you are making money online passively or actively, YouTube is a great way to make money. You can easily make money off your YouTube channel. For more information on how to make money off your YouTube channel, see the Section titled 'Ways to Make Money off Your YouTube Channel'.

STEPS TO STARTING A YOUTUBE CHANNEL

Starting a YouTube Channel is so easy that you can do it on your own. The following are the key steps you need to follow;

1. Create your YouTube Channel account
2. Upload your Channel art
3. Add your Channel descript plus other details
4. Verify your Channel

However, prior to starting these steps, you must have a Google Account. If you don't have one, you have to follow steps required to open one via Gmail.

Step 1: Create your YouTube Channel account

The first and foremost step in starting your YouTube channel is to create your YouTube Channel account.

a) Log into your Google account and then use it to log into YouTube. Once logged in, you will see the main menu on top left of the page shown as follows;

17

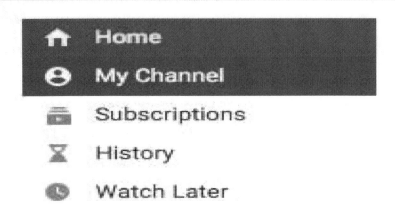

b) Click on 'My Channel' to get started. A pop window appears as shown below giving you an option of either creating a Personal Channel or a Business Channel.

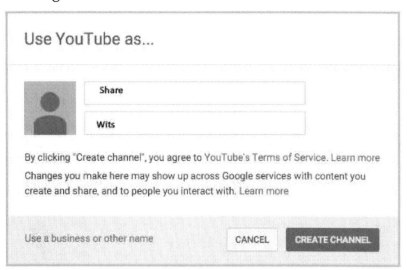

Creating a Personal Channel

c) If you want to create a Personal Channel, simply fill in the above window your First and Last names in the provided spaces and click on "CREATE CHANNEL' on the bottom right corner. The new Personal Channel will be created and you will be left with filling in Channel details.

Creating a Business Channel

d) However, if you want to create a Business Channel, click on the hyperlinked text that reads on the bottom right corner that reads "Use a business or other name". This will redirect you to a new dialog window as shown below;

You can now fill in your Business or other name in the space provided under "Name your channel", select appropriate category and click on "I agree to the Pages Terms". Finally, click on "Done" button to create your Business Channel.

19

Step 2: Upload your Channel Art

After successfully opening your YouTube Channel, you can now personalize it to your personal taste. First and foremost, give it a unique icon that can easily identify it and distinguish it from the crowd.

The Channel icon is found at the top-left corner of your Channel as shown below;

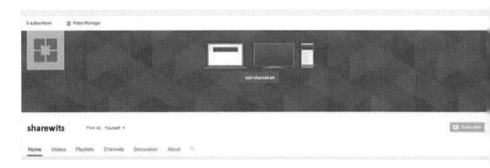

Once you insert your Channel icon, you can now upload and fix the main image – the Channel Art. This art image should have appropriate dimensions that would enable it to clearly appear on most gadget screens. YouTube recommends an art image to have a dimension of 2560 x 1440 pixels. For ease of loading, the file size must not exceed 4MB.

Step 3: Add Your Channel Description plus other details

Your channel has an 'About' section as shown below. This is the extreme right tab.

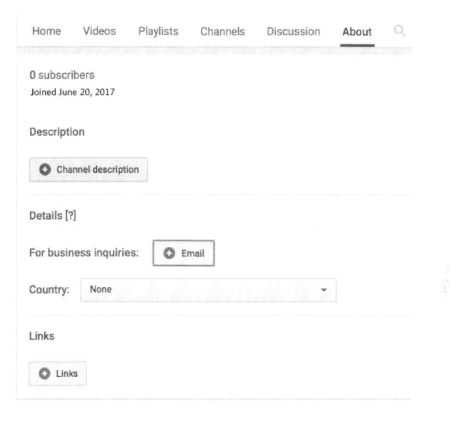

Under this section, you can describe to your audience what they expect to get from your channel.

Simply click on the "About" tab to open the About Page. Use the provision of 1000 words to write about you, about your channel and the nature of content you are going to provide to your audience.

There is also a provision to enter your contacts and your country. Furthermore, there is a link button which, when clicked, will open up a dialog box for you enter link details as shown below;

Using the 'Add' button, you can add up to five links. On the left side you enter the link name (e.g. Website, Twitter, Facebook, etc) and on the right side you enter the link's URL. Once you are finished, you can click on 'Done' button (extreme bottom-left corner) to update you link entries.

Step 4: Verify your YouTube Channel

Verifying your YouTube Channel allows YouTube to provide you with further customization and optimization facilities. These include Custom Thumbnails, Content ID, and external annotations, among a host of many other features.

To verify your YouTube Channel, while logged in, go to https://youtube.com/features, on top of the page that opens, you will see a 'Verify' button. When you click on the 'Verify' button, you will be prompted for a way which you want your YouTube Channel to be verified. You can either opt for call or text.

ITEMS NEED FOR A YOUTUBE RECORDING

YouTube is such a great platform for you to record and post your own videos. You don't have to be a professional expert to record your YouTube videos. You can easily learn on-the-job as you hone your skills. Nonetheless, you still need a good start-up point. Having good items for your video recording is a good way to start.

The following are the most essential items you need for a successful YouTube video recording;

1. Camera
2. Microphone
3. Stillness stand
4. Light source
5. Video editor
6. Computer

Camera

To begin with, you can use your laptop, tablet or Smartphone webcam. You can then advance on to external cameras.

For advanced options, please read the Section titled "How to Make Good Quality YouTube Videos".

Microphone

Modern Laptops, tablets and Smartphones come with in-built microphone. You can start off with these and then gradually move to more powerful external microphones.

For advanced options, please read the Section titled "How to Make Good Quality YouTube Videos".

Stillness stand

Tripod stand is the most widely used stillness stand. You need stillness for your video capture and setting up of an appropriate angle of capture. Nonetheless, with a laptop, you only need a table to start off.

For advanced options, please read the Section titled "How to Make Good Quality YouTube Videos".

Light source

Light is important in the clarity, contrast, color and richness of your video. Natural light is good to start with. However, there are certain places where natural light is not that sufficient. Thus, you need artificial lighting. Also there are situations where you want to have custom light effects. As an advanced professional, artificial light is easy to manipulate as opposed to natural light when you want to achieve sophisticated lighting effect.

For advanced options, please read the Section titled "How to Make Good Quality YouTube Videos".

Video editor

Once you have taken your video, you need to edit it for better quality. Video editing allows you to get rid of unwanted segments, enhance certain features and generally improve the quality of your video.

For advanced options, please read the Section titled "How to Make Good Quality YouTube Videos".

Computer

Obviously, to edit your video and upload it to your YouTube channel, you need a computer. This computer can be a desktop, a laptop, a tablet, or even a Smartphone. Probably you already have a computer or you can afford to buy one. In the event that you are financially in a bad position, you can take advantage of a good cybercafé.

For advanced options, please read the Section titled "How to Make Good Quality YouTube Videos".

WAYS TO MAKE MONEY OFF YOUR CHANNEL

The internet has changed the way people interact, exchange ideas, receive information and transact their business. Over 50% of the world's adult population has access to internet. This translates to over 3 billion people across the world. There is a rapid migration of populations to online presence. The advantage of internet is that it is not adversely restricted by geographic limits. It is truly a global village.

The money goes where the people are. The internet has become the new source of business, employment and earning passive income. If you are an artist or you would like to earn money through your audiovisual presentations, you no longer have to be at the mercy of Hollywood, Film Studio merchants, TVs, and other traditional merchants. YouTube has liberated you. It has set you free to unleash your creativity and let the kings (your audience) determine your fate. Ultimately, it your audience that pays! Cut-off the long channel of brokers, dealers and other money-suckers! Deal with your audience directly! YouTube makes this possible.

There are so many creative talents that would never have seen the light of the day if YouTube never existed. Thanks to YouTube that some of them are multi-million-dollar stars. You too can make it. All you need is to master the many ways to make money off your YouTube Channel. This book shows you how.

The following are the best ways to make money off your YouTube Channel;

1. Paid content
2. Advertisements
3. Direct service
4. Sale of downloadable content
5. Affiliate marketing
6. Fan funding

Paid content

YouTube has a paid content which can enable you to make money from your creative endeavors.

There are two types of content that you can earn off your channel;

- **Paid video** – This is where by you are paid by each and every individual video. You receive payment either from purchases or rentals.
- **Paid Channel** – This is where you are paid for your entire channel, including its content. You receive payment via subscription

There are three ways by which you can earn from paid content;

- Purchases – This is a form of paid video where audience buys the right to view the paid video perpetually. Thus, the buyer owns rights to the video and you as the provider have a duty to avail it.
- Rentals – This is a one-off paid video transaction where audience pays to view your video for a certain pre-determined period e.g. 48 hours or 72 hours.
- Subscriptions - This applies to a paid channel. The audience subscribes either on monthly or annual basis to get access to all your public videos.

Advertisements

You can monetize your video/channel through Google Adsense advertisement. This allows you to monetize views. To be able to do this, you will need to have a Google Adsense account and link up your YouTube Channel to it.

Affiliate marketing

For more information on Affiliate Marketing, please read the Section titled "Affiliate Marketing".

Fan Funding

For more information on fan funding, please read the Section titled "Fan Funding".

AFFILIATE MARKETING

Affiliate marketing is a kind of marketing system whereby one party (affiliate/publisher) promotes a product of another party (merchant/product creator) through an intermediary (affiliate network/platform) for a reward.

How to use your YouTube Channel to promote your Affiliate products;

1. Choose a niche
2. Register to an Affiliate Network Platform
3. Get Affiliate links
4. Create Product's video
5. Use Affiliate links in your YouTube Channel to market the affiliate products

Criteria for choosing your niche product

The following criteria will help you decide on the most appropriate product niche;

- Choose a product niche that aligns with your passion
- Choose a product niche that is available on your preferred affiliate network platform

- Choose a product that is profitable
- Choose a product that you can continue marketing in the long-term

Criteria for choosing the best affiliate marketing platform;

1. Reputation
2. Commission percentage
3. Range of products to market
4. Diversity of income streams
5. Payment terms
6. Terms of service

Get Affiliate links

Affiliate links are special links that you can use to hyperlink your content to particular affiliate products that you are marketing. These are unique links such that they contain a your particular affiliate ID and also the product ID for purposes of monitoring sales made through your affiliate marketing effort.

Create Product videos

There are two types of product videos that you can create for your affiliate marketing endeavor;

- Product features video
- How-To-(Use) product video

For more information on how to create videos, refer to our section titled "How to Make Good Quality Video" later on in this book.

Insert affiliate links into your content to market affiliate products

Once the affiliate network platform gives you affiliate links, you now hyperlink specific content in your YouTube channel using the links so that readers can possibly click on them to be directed to the affiliate product that you are marketing. You can put these links into your video description and even in the video itself as you explain.

FIVERR GIGS

Fiverr is a popular freelancing site where you can get great project offers (gig) for your specific project to be done for as low as $5. Most of the gigs are $5. Some are in its incremental depending on the complexity of the gig. $5 is the basic unit of measure at Fiverr.

Why Fiverr Gigs?

There are several reasons that make Fiverr one of the most preferred ways to get a freelancer. The following are the most important;

- Affordability – Compared to many other freelancing sites, Fiverr gigs are budget-friendly.
- Plenty of experienced freelancers – There are many experienced freelancers on gigs that are focused on what you want to be done
- Creative-oriented – Fiverr is favorably oriented towards creative projects. Thus, you are more likely to find gigs matching your YouTube project. You can easily find gigs matching your design work (such as artwork for your YouTube channel, e.g. icon, profile photo, etc), video introductions, video voice-overs, video editing, SEO, analytics, among others.

- Quick to find a match – Since gigs are described in terms of a project offer, you can easily find a gig matching your project. This helps you to cut down on time needed to find the right freelancer.

How to get the best out of Fiverr Gigs

Like other freelancing sites, Fiverr is simply an online job marketplace. Thus, it is up to you to find the right freelancer. Like meeting strangers, you have little knowledge about them except what their gigs describe. Thus, you need telling signs as to whether the gig is right for you or not. As a rule of thumb, avoid gigs that;

- Have SEO backlinks – This indicates that the gig provider is actually using the gig to marketing something else as opposed to getting a job.
- Have huge real social media audience – Gigs with huge social media audience means that they are not likely to be custom to your particular need. They could be agency gigs focused on mass production.
- Too much on offer than what a $5 can possible provide – When you see a gig offering too low a price for what you want to be done, you obviously have to be concerned about the quality of output. Yes, price speaks!

The following could be indicators of a good gig;

- Reasonably priced – not too cheap to be real. This means that the gig provider considers his/her service valuable to your needs.
- Basic tasks – Not so complex tasks such as financial planning and consultancy. Fiverr gigs are not for complex tasks. Thus, when you see a gig offering complex tasks such as consultancy and complex planning for $5, take care.

Apart from these telling signs, poor or non-specific communication can bring about a negative experience. It is important that your instructions are specific, detailed and clear about what you want from a gig. Misunderstanding of what you want is more likely to result into the freelancer delivering what you did not intend.

PATREON

For YouTube artists and entrepreneurs, Patreon is a platform that is favorably held in high regard.

What is Patreon?

Patreon is a membership YouTube video. It is a crowdfunding platform that allows video makers, artists, musicians, and podcasters, among others to earn rewards for their creative effort without necessarily relying on the traditional advertising system.

Why Patreon?

Patreon came to rescue those who could not be able to maximize their incomes through YouTube advertisements. It provides an alternative means where fans (patrons) - the customers, would directly pay for what they enjoy.

The challenge with YouTube-based advertisement model is that there is no incentive for fans to contribute towards your creative endeavor. Thus, video creators lose out on potential source of revenue/funding.

How does Patreon work?

Patreon is not strictly an income model but rather a Crowdfunding model. It operates on the concept that allows Patrons (the donors) to pledge donation towards a given creative project (your YouTube video). Thus, in essence, it is geared towards financing your project. However, in effect, what you get in excess of your funding endeavor (investment) becomes your income (rather profit).

Patreon pledges

Patrons pledge their donations towards Crowdfunding your YouTube video project. There are two options for pledging;

- One-off pledge – This is a pledge that is non-recurring. A patron can make it once or severally in undefined, unexpected or unpredictable pattern. Thus, the creator has no expectation of future pledges other than that which has been made.
- Subscription-based pledge – this is a pledge that is recurrent on a defined periodic basis. By default, the subscription-based pledge recurs on monthly basis.

How much does Patreon charge for its platform service?

Patreon charges 5% on all pledges made. There are more transaction charges depending on your choice of payment.

How to setup your Patreon account

The following are steps to setting up your Patreon Account;

1. Register
2. Describe who you are
3. Create your Patron page
4. Set your goals
5. Set rewards

Register

The first and foremost step is to register yourself on Patreon platform. You can register using either of the following two ways;

1. Using your social media account – Patreon provides a means by which you can sign in using your Facebook account. This is much quicker way compared to email.
2. Using your email account – You will need to enter and confirm your email account.

Describe who you are

Once you have successfully registered, the next step is to describe who you are. You will be required to provide details about;

- Your identity – Basically, your social media links and YouTube Channel link

- Your niche (specialty) – This includes information such as what you are creating, what you are being paid for, or simply what your category is. The following images shows the most common categories;

Create your Patreon page

After describing who you are, the next step is to create your Patreon page. Your Patreon Page has six tabs;

1. Settings – This is where you can advance or adjust setting you made immediately after registering.
2. About – This tab provides the 'About' section where you will be required to describe what your Patreon page is all about. This is the first section your Patrons will see. Thus, it should be carefully created to inspire them to help you achieve your intended goal.
3. Rewards – This tab provides you an opportunity to tell your potential patrons what is in store for them should they become your patrons. It is kind of a sales pitch. The following diagram depicts some of the suggested rewards (you can create your own unique rewards);

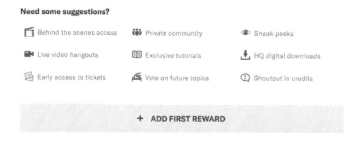

4. Goals – This tab provides you with an opportunity to let your patrons know what you aim to do when you achieve your set targets. There are two types of goals;

- Earning-based goals – this indicates what you intend to do when you hit a certain threshold of pledged earnings
- Community-based goals – this shows what you intend to do when you achieve a certain community target (e.g. number of patrons).

The following diagram depicts the two goals options;

What type of goal are you working towards?
You can change your mind at any time. You'll keep your Patreon earnings regardless of hitting your goals.

⦿ $ Earnings-based goals

Your goals are based on how much you earn on Patreon.

*"When I reach **$500 per month**, I'll start a special podcast series where I interview 1 patron every month."*

◯ ♣ Community-based goals

Your goals are based on how many patrons you have on Patreon.
Recommended for creators who've set their earnings number to private.

*"When I reach **500 patrons**, I'll hire an editor to help me release 2 videos per week instead of 1."*

+   ADD YOUR FIRST GOAL

5. Thanks - This tab provides you with a textbox (WYSWG text editor) where you will post your thank you message privately to your patrons.

6. Payments – This tab enables you to set the way you would like to be paid. This setting include;

   - How you will charge your patrons (e.g. type of pledge)
   - Your earnings visibility (e.g. whether your earnings should be visible to your patrons or not)
   - Payout settings (e.g. how you would like Patreon to send payments to you

The following diagram depicts the payment setting options;

Payment Schedule
Required

○ Monthly
Charge my patrons at the start of every month.

◉ Per Creation
Charge my patrons only when I make a Paid Post.

per blog post, MP3, video essay...

Earnings Visibility
Required

◉ 🌐 Public
Anyone who visits your page will see how much you earn per
null

○ 🔒 Private
Only you can see how much you earn. We'll hide your
earnings from your goals and the number of patrons
pledging at each reward tier.

Edit Payout Settings
learn more

Once your creator page is launched, you can edit your payout settings,
including how you'd like to get paid and your tax information.

Launching your Patreon page

Once you are done with creating and setting up your Patreon page, you are now ready to preview and launch it to the public. All you need is to click the big 'Preview and Launch' button that appears on the top-right corner of your page (immediately after the 'Payments' tab). This will launch a preview of your page. If you are not satisfied with it, you can go back and do further editing and refinement. However, if you are satisfied with the preview, you can go ahead click on 'Go Live' button (on top of the right panel) to launch it.

How to build your patron base

Building a patron base involves the following critical steps;

1. **Reach out** – You have to be known. Thus, you have to reach out to potential patrons so that they get to know you. Having free introductory video clips and some freebies to offer is a good way to attract attention. Creating this awareness requires publicity. Social media, advertisements, among others are some of the ways by which you can reach out to potential patrons.

2. **Engage** – Engaging your audience (both patrons and potential patrons) is what creates constant patronage. It is what builds a loyal following. It is what brings commitment to pledge.

3. **Explore** – It is important to know your audience well. You cannot turn your audience into patrons if you can't have a basic understanding of their taste and preference.

How to reach out to potential patrons

Reaching out to potential patrons is all about promotion (publicity). The following are some of the ways by which you can promote your presence;

- Advertisement - Paid seo (PPC), Social media PPC
- Email marketing
- Forum discussion
- Commenting on niche-related blogs
- Social media profile
- Youtube video posting
- Documenting and posting interview of an influential blogger
- Guest blogging

For details on this, please read the next section titled "Traffic to Your Website/Blog".

How to engage your audience and patrons

There are no shortcuts to engaging your audience and patrons. You have to give them attention. Responding to enquiries, answering questions and replying to comments is a great way to ensure that you stay engaged with them. For Patreons, having a chat or phone call helps to build trust and enhance loyalty. Be present. Be available. Serve.

How to explore your audience and patrons

The following are the three primary ways by which you can explore your audience and patrons in order to know them better;

- Polling
- Surveying
- Analyzing

Polling

Set up a poll on your blog or social media platform. Polling works well when there are potentially multiple standard responses which can be categorized into options.

Polling can be applied when you want people to rate an idea or specific performance (e.g. of your video clip). It can also be used when you want to know certain basic preferences of your audience or patrons.

You can set up a poll on your blog or social media platform. WordPress has great polling plugins. Joomla and Drupal too have them. When it comes to Social Media platforms, Facebook and Twitter have polling apps which you can use.

Surveying

Surveys are great when it comes to getting deeper custom details that cannot be availed via polling options. There are several survey tools out there that you can use for this endeavor.

WordPress has such plugins. Google Forms has such facility. You can also have independent survey apps such as SurveyMonkey, Zoho Survey, Survey Gizmo, among others.

Analyzing

When it comes to analyzing, demographics become the most important of all analyses that you need to make. You need to know demographic factors such as;

- Location – Location density is important in helping you focus your attention. Location grouping can help you make location-specific offers. It can also give you a glimpse of culture, purchasing power, among others.

- Gender – People of different gender have different perceptions and responses. Thus, it is important to know the dominant gender of your patrons either as a whole or per specific product (video)

- Age group – Like gender, age group is also a sensitive issue. In fact, it is more sensitive than gender and locality. Each age group, irrespective of location and gender has certain specific tastes and preferences. You need to know what age group that you appeals to most so that you can properly focus your attention.

- Etc – There are many other demographic factors that you may require analyzing depending on your particular need.

<u>Youtube Analytics</u>, already provided in your YouTube Channel as part of your <u>Creator Studio</u>, can help you analyze the performance of your particular video.

TRAFFIC TO YOUR WEBSITE/BLOG

There are many ways to generate traffic for your website. The following are some of the ways by which you can direct traffic to your blog;

- Advertisement - Paid SEO (PPC), Social media PPC
- Email marketing
- Forum discussion
- Commenting on niche-related blogs
- Social media profile
- Youtube video posting
- Documenting and posting interview of an influential blogger
- Guest blogging

Advertisement

If you have a high quality YouTube video, you can optimize revenue by advertising it so that you can quickly earn enough to finance your next YouTube video project. Time is money. The quicker you earn the faster you can launch the next process thus accelerating the income multiplier effect.

There are two prominent ways to advertise your YouTube video online;

1. Paid SEO
2. Social Media PPC

Paid SEO

Paid SEO refers to driving traffic to your website by use of Keywords which are paid for. The keywords could be the same organic keywords (see Section titled "How to Keyword Optimize YouTube Titles and Descriptions" for more details on organic keywords). The only difference is that, you pay a Search Engine provider to rank your web page on YSRP based on user queries that relate to your keywords. Thus, the ranking is not organic but advertised.

Social Media PPC

PPC stands for Pay per Click. This is the most common form of online advertising whereby adverts are strategically placed in user access points to draw their attention. Facebook is the most commonly used Social media for PPC. When you log into Facebook there are certain adverts that appear on the sidebars and sometimes together with feeds. These are PPC adverts.

You can pay Facebook to render such PPC adverts on your behalf.

Email Marketing

Email marketing refers to use of email to drive traffic to your website. You can create content with targetable links to your web page and send to various email addresses based on potential leads. When the targeted leads get impressed by the content, they click on the links provided within the emailed content which leads them to your web page.

To inspire readers of your email to clink on your link, send them a demo video or an animation that can play within their email. It has to be short but compelling enough to make them click on that link.

Forum Discussion

Forums are a great way to draw traffic to your website. You simply find forums that are relevant to your video niche and subscribe to them. Afterwards, you can offer relevant advice or opinion on a topical issue and provide your credentials (including your name and YouTube link) so that those who desire more information can access it.

If you are known to the Forum administrator, you can request to post a demo video or animation for maximum impact.

Commenting on niche-related videos

Just like Forum discussion, make a list of your niche-related authority YouTube Channels. Post helpful and inspiring comments relevant to the video. At the end of the comment, offer your video as backup support (include link to your YouTube Video).

Social media profile

Having a social media profile is a great way to engage your audience. LinkedIn, Google Plus, Quora Facebook and Twitter are great place to derive traffic via your social media profile. The first four are extremely helpful if you are offering professional services (such as content writing, SEO, etc).

Post demo video clip on your Social media profile advising your audience to click on the link to view full video.

Documenting and posting interview of an influential video blogger

Every niche has an influential video blogger, that is, a video blogger who has a huge loyal following. An influential video blogger can help you gain a significant volume of traffic, especially if you are relatively new entrant with quality content and valued service addition. Simply invite an influential blogger to an interview. A video-recorded interview (that you will also transcribe) is the best option. Request the influential blogger to inform his/her audience about the interview on his/her YouTube

Channel and provide links to your video where the interview video and/or verbatim transcription are. This way, the influencer's audience will become aware of your YouTube Channel and will trust it based on the authority of the influential video blogger.

Guest Video Blogging

Guest video blogging refers to registering to send video posts to authority YouTube channels on topical issues that you are expert in. The primary aim of guest video blogging is to have an opportunity to expose yourself and your YouTube Channel and gain valuable backlinks to your Channel.

FAN FUNDING

Fan funding has become the most preferred way for startup creators to fund their creative projects. You too can achieve great success in funding your YouTube startup project.

YouTube recognized the need for startup creators to receive funding for their creative video projects. Thus, it created a Fan Funding facility for this. However, in the early parts of year 2017, YouTube decided to discontinue its Fan Funding facility. Thus, in this section, it is of no use for us to dwell on an already discontinued facility. Nonetheless we will focus on the concept itself. Fan Funding!

While YouTube discontinued its Fan Funding facility, it replaced it with a unique facility that still retained the concept but with new features and a totally different approach. This facility is known as Super Chat. We will explore Super Chat and other fan funding options, some of them outside the YouTube ecosystem. Conceptually, Patreon is a fun funding facility.

In this section, we are going to consider two categories of fan funding platforms;

- YouTube-based fan funding platforms
- Non-YouTube fan funding platforms

YouTube-based fan-funding platform – Super Chat

These are fan-funding platforms either established by YouTube or relies on YouTube infrastructure. So far, Super Chat is the fan funding facility provided by YouTube.

How to get Super Chat

To get Super Chat on your Channel, you must meet the following eligibility criteria;

1. Be a resident of the qualified countries
2. Have a fan base of at least 1,000 subscribers

How to get started with Super Chat

Once signed in to your YouTube channel, go to youtube.com/features and select 'Enable' under Super Chat

How fans make payment using Super Chat

It is good to know how you receive Super Chat funds from fans. The following are the key steps to making a Super Chat purchase;

1. Select the '$' sign within a live chat
2. Select 'Send a Super Chat'
3. Choose an amount to pay from the list
4. Enter the Super Chat message (optional)

5. Select 'Buy and Send'
6. Complete the transaction

Advantages of Super Chat

1. It is easy to use
2. Has a bigger country reach than its predecessor (Fan Funding). Currently available in slightly over 40 countries
3. It boosts live streaming revenue
4. It gives preference to the dollar audience (paying audience)
5. Fans enjoy a prominent status as their Super Chat is ranked above the rest.
6. The special color highlight of the Super Chat enables you to give the Super Chat fun a fast and quick attention
7. It promotes interaction and engagement with more yielding fans
8. It has a robust admin analytics facility that can enable you monitor your Super fans and be able to grant them special appreciation in a private way.

Disadvantages of Super Chat

1. You can only use it in live streaming
2. It has no annotations
3. You must have a fan base of at least 1,000 subscribers
4. YouTube get a big chunk of bite of your pie. Yes, YouTube gets 30% of your revenue

Non-YouTube fan funding platforms

Why use non-YouTube fan funding platforms? First of all, using non-YouTube fan funding platforms doesn't necessarily mean that you won't utilize all facilities availed by YouTube (including Super Chat). It simply means that you are seeking to expand funding alternatives so as to increase project funding. You can still run your project on YouTube and Patreon. Furthermore, most of these non-YouTube platforms are for funding pre-launching costs. As such, they are capital-based as opposed to revenue-based. Yet, you can still use YouTube for publicity demos and appeals towards your funding projects on these platforms. This is a much more effective approach.

There are two types of non-YouTube fan funding platforms;

- Music-specific fan funding platforms
- General fan funding platforms

Music-specific fan funding platforms

These are platforms that specifically support music artists. The following are the two most popular music-specific fan funding platforms;

- <u>PledgeMusic</u> – This is an all-or-nothing fan funding platform. You create a fan funding project and launch it with a specific funding target. If your funding target is met, you get all the funds (thus, you get all). However, if the funding target is not met, you refund (thus, you get nothing) your backers (pledged fans).

- <u>ArtistShare</u> – This is by far the oldest Crowdfunding and fan funding platform. It has had a reputation of the highest Grammy Award winners who have been fan funded. Unlike PledgeMusic, you keep what has been raised, whether you meet your funding target or not. It has a separate launch platform known as <u>FanFunded</u> where you can go directly and launch your project.

General fan funding platforms

These platforms support all kinds of creative projects. However, they are more oriented towards Crowdfunding (where non-fans can fund) than specifically fan funding. The following are the three most popular;

- <u>Kickstarter</u> – Kickstarter is by far the most popular Crowdfunding platform. Unlike Indiegogo, Kickstarter has three main limitations – (1) You must achieve your goal (funding target), and (2) The goal must be achieved within the deadline. If either or both of the two conditions are not met, pledges are returned to the backers. Thus, it is an 'all-or-nothing' kind of funding platform. Furthermore, the third and major limitation is that project owners must be residents of the United States. Thus, funding is only available to US residents, and not just US residents but those with a Social Security number. Knowing that over 70% of YouTube creators reside outside US, this is a very major limitation.

- Indiegogo – Indiegogo is far more flexible than Kickstarter. It seeks to overcome the three limitations of Kickstarter. Thus, (1) You don't have to achieve your goal (funding target) for funds to be released, (2) There is reasonable deadline, and (3) It is available to project creators across the world. However, it has a fixed (Kickstarter-like) or flexible funding option. Indiegogo is simply hybrid.

- GoFundMe – GoFundMe, unlike Kickstarter, it is specifically for non-commercial endeavors. It is used to fund projects for a cause. It could be charity or personal expenses such as education cost, medical expenses, etc.

Thus, if you want to fund YouTube projects that targets charity causes, you can use it.

SHARING YOUR KNOWLEDGE WITH TUTORIALS

Knowledge is wealth. Yet, the greatest challenge that faces many is how to convert this wealth into money so that they can afford their livelihoods and be adequately rewarded for their wealth. You can monetize your knowledge. Yes, convert your wealth into liquidity. YouTube is one such platform where you can monetize your knowledge.

The good thing with knowledge is that the more you share it the more its value goes up. Of what use would it be if you don't utilize it? None! Share your knowledge. Demonstrate it out. Serve others. YouTube is a great platform for you to achieve this. How?

How to share your knowledge using YouTube

Tutorials, more specifically, "How-to" tutorials have become the most popular way of learning on the internet. The internet has expanded the learning space beyond the brick-and-mortar classrooms. You have something to teach. What you could think is so obvious isn't obvious to all. Someone somewhere is desperately looking for that knowledge that you have. Simply create video tutorials practically demonstrating your knowledge to others, and you will be in for great rewards.

Why video tutorials are easier for anyone to make

Video tutorials, unlike other tutorials, don't require much of your presence. The focus is primarily on what it is than who you are. You need not complex environment but a simple, clean, uncluttered and organized environment for your video shootout. Actually, if your tutorials are intangible in nature (such as lectures), a desk, probably a white board (if you are going to write something), a computer (preferably a laptop), webcam, microphone, video recording and video editing software are the basic tools that you need.

In case you going to offer lessons where you have to create a physical object or use a physical object for demonstration purposes, e.g. craftwork, gadget assembly, cooking, machine usage demos, lab demos, etc, then, you need slightly more advanced equipment than the webcam and microphone provided by the laptop. You will need a mounted camera, button microphone, light source, and other scene-based video shootout equipment.

What skills you need

The most important skills need to properly deliver your tutorials are;

1. Communication skills – You must be able to communicate effectively to learners. First, you must communicate in a language that your target learners understand. Secondly, you must be able to present your tutorials in such a way that they are easily digestible. Third, you should be able to answer all potential questions within your tutorials since the communication is one-way – from the tutor to the learner. Fourth, you must be able to properly use your tone such that a learner can easily discern when you are emphasizing an important point. Lastly, communication should flow naturally. Yes, you shouldn't animate your communication.

2. Interpersonal relationship skills – While the physical interaction is not two-way, you should communicate in such a way that makes the learner feels at ease and relaxed. It should make the learner feel that this is important. In case you are focused, your body language should be warm, friendly, comforting and welcoming.

3. Presentation skills – Though part of communication, presentations skills can be enhanced by the way you use

your presentation tools. A good mastery of slide presentations, diagrammatic expressions, highlighting, use of bullets, among others, makes it easy for learners to grasp your concepts. Another core element of presentation skills is pacing and timing. How you time various elements of your presentation and how you pace them will increase or decrease content absorption by the learners. It is not uncommon to find presentations that run faster than a learner can read them. It is prudent to practice first in dummy classrooms (e.g. making a presentation to your friends) so that you can gauge and set your timing and pacing before uploading the final product on YouTube. Feedback from your friends will help you adjust appropriately. Let your video tutorial be reviewed by them and other people of interest (more so, those who have successfully done the same) before you deem it a final product.

4. Expert skills – You have to demonstration professionalism and expertise in your core area. It is not that your tutorials should be based on a complex subject such rocket science or nuclear engineering. No! Even if it is about 'how to feed a baby', 'how to clean a loo', 'how to peel an orange', or such other kinds of tutorials, you have to demonstrate that you know something beyond the ordinary about that topic. Yes, something that can add value to the learner.

5. Professional skills – Well, expert skills and professional skills are often used interchangeably. Though apparently synonymous, they hardly mean one and the same thing. You can have expert skills yet poor professional skills. Professional skills are more about how you project yourself while executing your expertise. Professional skills include such things as proper etiquette, ethics, and integrity, among others. Professional skills inspire learners to emulate you. They project a sense of respect and nobility. This brings an appreciation what you are doing in the minds of the learners. This helps them feel that 'you are worth what you are doing' as opposed to merely 'what you are doing is worth'.

Feedback responses

It is important that you request for feedback from learners (via YouTube comments) and be able to review and respond appropriately. This will help you understand and appreciate what learners are looking for. This can help you create an improved version (which you ought to make) or have better skills for the next video tutorial project.

However, not all feedbacks are helpful or done in good faith. Some can even be insults. If you can't respond to them in a more positive and tolerant manner, better ignore them. Yet, don't keep abusive comments on your Channel. Simply delete them as fast as you detect them. They are infectious germs that you ought not to let them infect others.

LOCAL MARKETING AGENCY

Marketing is a great way of ensuring that your concept satisfies the intended consumer. Thus, a local marketing agency is simply an agency whose engagement is to ensure that a creator's concept satisfies the intended target within a certain given locality.

For a concept to satisfy a consumer, it must have utility;

- Utility of form – It must be in the right form, i.e. product (e.g. good or service)
- Utility of place – It must be delivered at the right place
- Utility of time – It must be delivered at the right time

In line with the 4P's of marketing (Product, Place, Price, Promotion), a local marketing agency must;

- Help its client bring forth a **product** – this involves identification, selection and conversion of a concept into a product (e.g. a product feature YouTube video)
- Helps its client establish a distribution channel (e.g. your YouTube Channel) to reach the customer's **place** (e.g. YouTube platform)

- Help its client determine the product's **price** – In essence, price is a value that customer receives which he/she would be willing to reward.
- Help its client develop and implement appropriate **promotion** strategy – This promotion strategic includes publicity (advertisements, etc), enticements (offers, discounts, etc), among others.

Should you need or form a local marketing agency?

This depends on your needs and expertise. If you are an expert marketer, your knowledge gained in this book can help you create a local marketing agency for clients seeking to market their videos on YouTube platform. On the other hand, if you are a product creator who is not a marketing expert, you would probably need a local marketing agency to help you market your product. It all depends on whether you want to be a marketer or a marketing client.

Becoming a local marketing agency

Becoming a local marketing agency for YouTube video products is not such a hard endeavor if you are already a trained marketer. All you need is to grasp what is provided in this book and customize to your own skills and expertise. For those without marketing skills, you need to take up a marketing course and then top-up with what is provided in this book.

Hiring a local marketing agency

The remainder of this section will focus on you as a client desiring to engage the services of a local marketing agency.

Why hire a local marketing agency?

The following are key reasons as to why you would want to hire a local marketing agency

- Lack of expertise
- Lack of time
- Desire to automate (for more information on automation, see our last section titled "How to Grow Your Channel)

What to look for in your local marketing agency

It is highly likely that, should you choose to advertise to hire a local marketing agency, there will be many who will respond to your call. Thus, it is important to get the best. The following criteria will help you get the best local marketing agency for your project;

- Reputation – A reputable local marketing agency will be quick to provide you with verifiable projects portfolio. Vouch through the profile of each of the prospective agencies to rank the best. A reputable agency will allow you to contact some of its clients for you to verify details of their portfolio.

- Expertise – Expertise is closely associated with reputation. However, an agency could be reputable yet not be an expert in your specific project. Thus, you need to evaluate whether the agency has sufficient experience, skilled staff and adequate resources to undertake your project. Look at the experience of people who run the marketing to see if they are true experts.

- Value – What value does the prospective agency promise to give? At what cost? You need to carry out some basic cost-benefit analysis to find out an agency that is not just reputable, not only has the required expertise but also grants you optimal value for your every dollar sacrificed.

How to evaluate the success of your marketing agency

Once you hire your local marketing agency, it doesn't end there. You must establish the expected deliverables. To do this, you need to factor the following;

- Benchmarking – Do benchmarking, that is, establish a standard of expectation. If you have samples of what you consider to be the best projects so far, share that with your agency and discuss it so that your agency knows the basic minimum that you expect. Ascertain whether your agency is capable of meeting those bare minimum or, even capable of exceeding expectations. If possible, benchmarking should be part of prequalification process.

- Goal-setting – Have a discussion with your marketing agency to set goals and targets of expected deliverables.
- Result – Monitor delivery of the project at every stage. You should have milestones based on targets so that you can easily monitor result and take appropriate remedial action when the outcome doesn't meet your expectations.

How to reward your local marketing agency

Rewarding your marketing agency is a crucial element of your marketing endeavor. The reward is not just a compensation for sacrifice made but also a motivation to achieve greater outcome. You have to balance out the two without sacrificing either.

Your reward should be based on the following criteria;

- Goal-oriented – The reward should be based on achieved goals
- Target-specific – Reward should be based on achieved targets (milestones)
- Result-based – Reward should be based not on effort or performance but results

- Bonus-based – Instead of fixed costs, offer bonus only and only if the expected targets are achieved or superseded.

Ideally, the lower the fixed marketing cost, the lower the risk. Thus, avoid fixed rewards as much as you can.

HOW TO MAKE GOOD QUALITY YOUTUBE VIDEOS

We had discussed "Items Needed for a YouTube Recording" in the first sections of this book. We now have to build on that and see how to use those items (and more enhanced ones) to make good quality videos.

The following are important steps to high quality YouTube videos;

1. Have the right equipment at hand
2. Choose a video concept
3. Setup the shooting scene
4. Shoot the video
5. Refine your video
6. Review your video
7. Upload your video on YouTube

Have the right equipment at hand

To recap, the following are the most essential items you need for a successful YouTube video recording;

1. Camera

2. Microphone
3. Stillness stand
4. Light source
5. Video editor
6. Computer
7. Enhancements (optional)

Camera

For quality video, you need to invest in a better camera. The following are two popular options;

- Canon EOS 5D Mark II
- Canon EOS Rebel T5

You can choose other models that you like (mostly from Canon or Nikon) that can measure up to the two mentioned or better. The most important thing is that your choice camera must be at least a DSLR (Digital Single-Lens Reflex). Also, choose a camera that you can operate. A sophisticated camera that is too complex for you to operate is of no benefit to you.

Microphone

For high quality video, you need a good standalone dedicated microphone. Why standalone? This is important for high quality video. When your microphone is attached to other EMI (Electromagnetic Interference) devices such as camera or laptop, there is noise and background echo.

You don't have to go for very expensive microphone, the following two types or their equivalents can do;

- Audio-Technica ATR 3350
- Rhode VideoMic

Stillness stand

Depending on your setup, you may need two tripod stands – for the camera and for the microphone. However, if you can find a place to mount either or both of the two, that will work fine. But, if you intend to change shooting scenes for more projects, you will need to eventually have the tripod stands.

You may also need stillness stand for anchoring light source and other necessary gadgets.

Light source

Light is important for quality video shooting. You may require different light quality depending on your preferred shooting scene setup. Ideally there should be three light sources (see video shooting scene setup for more information). A simple LED lamp with masked screen (or diffusion paper) in front (to spread the light) can work.

You can get an LED lamp with the following specifications;

- 80w
- 800 lumens
- Natural day-light warmth (light temperature)
- Dimmable

These specifications are for guideline only. With experience, you will find the most appropriate specifications to suit your particular shooting environment and desired lighting effects.

Video editor

Once you've made a shooting, you require video editor to refine your video. The following are some of the video editing software that you can use;

- Lightworks (PC only)
- Adobe Premiere
- Pinnacle Studio 20 Ultimate
- Apple Final Cut Pro X (Mac only)

There are many others out there. Just choose the one you are comfortable working on.

Computer

A good laptop is the best.

Choose a video concept

Every product that has ever been produced starts from a concept. A concept is an idea that you have in mind that will shape your product creation. Your concept should outline each and every stage of your shooting.

The best way to ensure that your video will be easily editable and refined is to use the'jump-cuts' technique. In this technique, a video is built up from dozens to hundreds of small clips.

The following steps will ensure that your video concept is properly implemented using jump-cut technique;

1. Write down a script expressing your video concept
2. Edit your script so that it breaks down into short sentences
3. Make cuts (blocks of sentences) each fitting into one clip. This could be one sentence or two or three). A block must be easy to memorize.
4. Describe an image clip for each cut
5. Arrange the cuts to follow each other sequentially

Set up the shooting scene

Once you have created your video concept, now setup your shooting scene. The following are key components that you ought to arrange in your scene

1. The object (the focus of your shooting)

2. The camera
3. The microphone
4. The light source
5. Helper(s)' position(s)

The object (in artistic sense) is that live scene that needs to be captured. It could be you, or some other object under consideration. If it is you, then the microphone will need to be closer to you with the camera facing you. Helpers should be in the invisible background.

The most complex part of arranging the shooting scene is lighting. For a good effect, you need at least three sources of light;

1. Main light
2. Fill light
3. Background light

The following should be the layout of your lighting;

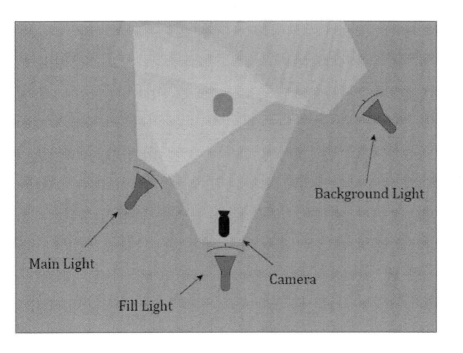

Main Light

Fill Light

Camera

Background Light

However, if natural light is adequate, you can utilize it.

The following layout, in case of natural light, can also do;

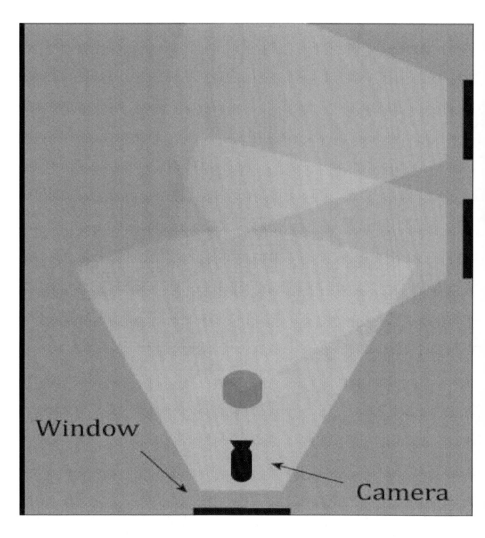

Shooting the video

With proper shooting scene, you can now go ahead and shoot your video. The best way to shoot the video is to do it in clips. To appear more natural, you will need a helper in the background to read for you the script for each clip as you repeat it for video shootout. If you are alone, it means you will keep posing every other time to read. However, this won't appear natural. The alternative is to pre-record you audio clips and then re-play each clip one a time as you repeat it for video recording.

Refine your video

Once you are done with recording clips, the next step is to use your video editing software to refine your video. In this process, you will need to do the following;

1. Edit out unwanted sound – This include your helper's sound or pre-recorded sound
2. Edit out unwanted image segments – In case you don't have a helper, it is most likely that your camera will capture you while reading the script or switching on and off the record player. You will have to remove these.
3. Review your video clips – It will be good to let a friend to go through the clips so that you can have better perspective. If possible, involve more people. Yes, the video is not for you but your audience. How your friends and loved ones perceive it could be a hint of how your audience out there will perceive it. Incorporate their recommendations if you feel they are great. Most

importantly, don't ignore their input as they are your first audience.

4. Merge the clips for a smooth flow – Merge the clips to form a single flowing video.

5. Do final touches – Final touches include lighting effects, sound effects, among others.

Upload the video to your YouTube channel

Once you are done with everything else, you are now ready to go. Yes, upload your great video onto your YouTube channel.

Optimize your YouTube Video

Once you have uploaded your video on YouTube, the next step is to optimize it. See the next section titled "How to Keyword Optimize YouTube Titles and Descriptions" for more optimization details.

HOW TO KEYWORD OPTIMIZE YOUTUBE TITLES AND DESCRIPTIONS

Keywords are specific text tags relied on by YouTube Search Engine to search and rank results on the YouTube Search Results Page (YSRP).

Why are Keywords such important in SEO?

Keyword is the language of identifiers by search engines. These are the pointers used by the surfer to direct search engine hooks.

When the user places a search query, the user may or may not know the web page that he/she is looking for. For example, when I want to find videos where I can learn about Youtube SEO, I simply go to youtube.com and type 'Youtube seo' as shown in the diagram below;

Youtube search engine will attempt to match the search query with the keywords in the content, index and rank the content onto YSRP if the search query and content keywords match.

What are suggested keywords?

Suggested keywords are those keywords that come in a dropdown list below your search keyword in the search engine.

For example, in our case, the primary keyword is 'youtube seo'. YouTube search engine suggests the following keywords on its dropdown list;

youtube seo **tutorial**
youtube seo **video**
youtube seo **tips**
youtube seo **guide**
youtube seo **bangla**
youtube seo **tools**
youtube seo **optimization 2017**
youtube seo **tips bangla**
youtube seo **telugu**

Why are suggested keywords such important?

More often than not, when you are doing keyword research, you only have an idea of the primary keyword (for example, 'youtube seo'). The primary keyword, though important, is too general. It only helps to lead to the other keywords that are more specific. For example, if your video is about teaching people YouTube SEO, then, you are better off opting for;

- Youtube seo tutorial
- Youtube seo guide
- Youtube seo tips

These are more specific than 'youtube seo' for your Youtube seo tutorial video.

What are the primary, secondary and long-tail keywords?

Taking our example above 'youtube seo' is a primary keyword. All the suggested keywords (though some may not be relevant) are secondary keywords. Secondary keywords are simply those keywords that are related to (or are alternatives to) the primary keyword.

What is the difference between short-tail and long-tail keywords?

Quantitatively, short-tail keywords basically have two to three words. Qualitatively, they are not detailed enough to describe user's needs and benefits.

On the other hand, quantitatively, long-tail keywords have more than three keywords. Qualitatively, long-tail keywords describe the user's particular need or benefit.

For example:

- "Youtube SEO" is a short-tail keyword. This keyword doesn't describe a particular need or benefit. The secondary keywords we have seen above are all short-tail keywords.

- "How to optimize YouTube videos" is a long-tail keyword. This keyword describes a user's particular need of "optimizing Youtube videos".

- "How to make money from YouTube videos" is also a long-tail keyword. This keyword describes a user's particular need of "Making Money from Youtube videos".

The most important dividing line between short-tail and long-tail keywords is not necessarily quantitative but largely qualitative. Just having many words jumbled up together without any identifiable need or benefit doesn't make it a long-tail keyword.

Selecting your best short-tail keywords

The best short-tail keywords are those that are;

1. Relevant to your video
2. Have high search volume
3. Have long-term positive trend

We've seen how to get suggested (secondary) keywords. We've also seen how to select relevant short-tail keywords from the suggested keywords. The next important step is to find keywords that;

- Have high search volume – High search volume indicates that many people are searching for that particular kind of content. You can use <u>Google Keyword Planner</u> to enable you choose which among the relevant keywords has high search volume.

- Have long-term positive trend – You obviously desire to continue earning for long from your Youtube investment. In this regard, it is important to create evergreen videos. That is, videos that can remain relevant to viewers for a long period of time. To support this, you will need also to use keywords that have a long-term positive trend. That is keywords that have been used, continue to be used and have prospects of being used in the long-term future. <u>Google Trends</u> is such a great tool to help you determine among your relevant keywords which of them has long-term positive trend.

Selecting your best long-tail keywords

Just as short-tail keywords, you can also get suggested long-tail keywords using the same methods. For example, in our case, the following are our long-tail keywords;

1. "How to optimize YouTube videos"

2. "How to make money from YouTube videos"

For the first long-tail keyword, the following are suggested long-tail keywords;

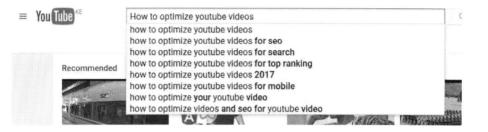

For the second long-tail keyword, the following are suggested long-tail keywords;

Just as the short-tail keywords, the following are criteria for selecting the best long-tail keyword;

1. Relevance to your video
2. High search volume
3. Long-term positive trend

You can use the same methodology and tools used to select the best short-tail keywords to get the best long-tail keywords.

Why you must include keyword in your YouTube titles

YouTube search engines use your title as the first landing point in seeking data that can rank your video. Having keyword in your title boosts this ranking in the YSRP.

To optimize this ranking:

- Preferably, use long-tail keyword. If not possible (maybe due to length or lack of fitness to the title), you can use the primary keyword or appropriate secondary keyword (if that makes the title sound/rank better).
- Have a title neither too short nor too long. An optimal title is between 40 and 50 words. If the title has more words than 50 words, the rest are more likely going to be truncated which hurts the readability. If the title has shorter than 40 words, then you are losing on optimization as the search engine would like to gather as more meaningful data as possible that matches the surfer's search query in order to rank your video.

Why you must include long-tail keywords in your Youtube description

Long tail keywords, as illustrated above, help to isolate a particular entity from a crowd of others. They help the search engine to be more precise.

The following are important reasons as to why you should consider long-tail keywords in your SEO campaign;

- **They are less competitive** – Short-tail keywords are usually competitive, that is, there are many websites competing to deliver the package queried (demanded) by the user. Thus, the probability of your package being indexed on the SERP is minimal. On the other hand, long-tail keywords are less competitive. This is because they are more precise (relatively high-grade) and thus fewer websites are competing to deliver queried package.

- **They bring more serious leads** – Most ecommerce experts will tell you that long-tail keywords experience higher conversion rate than short-tail keywords. Why? This is simply because users who employ long-tail keywords in their search query are more serious and particular of exactly what they want – a particular need or benefit. Thus, they are more likely to respond positively to the package they are offered (e.g. reading, making a buy decision, consulting further, etc)

- **They have lower bounce rates** – Bounce rates refer to the rate at which visitors leave without having been welcomed or having decided to take what is offered. It is like a stranger bumping into a wrong room or entering a wrong street and bounces back in haste. Due to long-tail keywords being more specific, bounce rates are low. A history of high bounce rates lowers your page ranking and visibility since the search engines get tired of keeping on presenting the wrong package to visitors. High bounce rates hurt your SEO.

- **They have relatively higher conversion rate** – Obviously, more serious leads (e.g. potential audience, potential buyers, etc) have higher conversion rate (yielding positive results e.g. sales, loyal audience, more following, etc) compared to less serious leads.

- **They have relatively higher yield** – It is always the intent of any rational person to get the most maximum benefit out of the least possible sacrifice. For example, if you have one video that has 500,000 visitors per day; it is far cheaper and much more beneficial compared to a Youtube channel that has 50 videos that yields the same number of visitors per day. On the other hand, having videos that have 1,000 visitors per day of which 100 of them make a buy decision is far more beneficial than having a video with 5,000 visitors per day only for less than 50 of them to make a buy decision. The high number of visits is important (most probably due to use of short-tail keywords) but a higher yield is much more important (most probably due to use of long-tail keywords).

How to apply long-tail keyword in your description

The following are the three important sections of your description where you must position your long-tail keyword for optimal effect;

- First paragraph – Search engines give more importance to the first paragraph than any other paragraph when it comes to search, indexing and ranking.
- Middle – To establish validity of your content to the search query, the search engine seeks how many other times has your long-tail keyword been used. Using it once in the middle is strategic in this regard.
- Last paragraph – The last paragraph is considered as the conclusive paragraph, search engine considers it too for emphasis purposes (just to assure itself that 'this is it!').

Also, use primary and secondary keywords 1-3 times in the description. To avoid your description from being considered as keyword stuffed by search engines, reduce keyword density by making your content as long as possible but within the 1000-word maximum limit.

HOW TO GROW YOUR CHANNEL

To grow your YouTube channel, you need not only scale it up as a revenue source but also boost it as a traffic source.

Scaling up your YouTube Channel

Scaling up your YouTube Channel simply means expanding its capacity to generate more revenue.

The following are some of the ways to scale up your YouTube Channel

- Cross-selling
- Up-selling
- Collaboration
- Cameo appearances
- Fan Funding
- Automation

Cross-Selling

Cross-selling refers to the process of providing additional complementary products that can improve the utility of the product being sold. For example you can create a 'How to Make a

95

Kimono Skirt' video. Along it, you can give your audience a affiliate link to buy a hat that goes with Kimono Skirt or make them view your other video on 'How to Make a Kimono Matching Hat'.

Up-Selling

Up-selling refers to the process of providing higher value alternatives to the product being sold. Up-selling is commonly applied when it comes to freemiums (commonly applied to apps, eBooks and subscriptions). For example, you can create a free app with limited features and create another premium app with advanced features. While you are offering and demonstrating to your audience how to get and use your free app, you also encourage them to buy your premium app should they want these extra features that would make their experience much better.

Up-selling is also commonly applied in Smartphones, Cars, machines, equipment and many other kind of items which you can sell at different grades.

Collaboration

Collaboration is where two content writers marshal their efforts towards a creative venture. The following are some of the ways you can collaborate;

- Letting another creator within your niche post a video on your channel and/or you doing the same on the other creator's channel
- Working together to produce a video
- Appearing as a guest video blogger on another creator's channel and vice versa.

Cameo appearances

Cameo appearance is simply an appearance by a well-known artist in your video so as to boost its visibility. This can be worded in the form of "featuring artist X". Cameo appearances raises attention of loyal fans of the artist making a cameo appearance and channels it to your video.

Fan Funding

Fan funding is a great way not only to earn an income but also to raise capital for your next video venture. This enables you to upscale your YouTube Channel by having more and higher quality videos.

For more information on fan funding, please read our earlier section titled 'Fan Funding'.

Automation

You have to appreciate that when you are starting, you will most likely work for money. But, to grow big, you will have to stop letting money employ you. Instead, you will have to start employing money - thus, letting money work for you. The best way to let money work for you is to automate your YouTube Channel.

The following are some of the ways by which you can automate your YouTube Channel;

- Outsource management of your Channel – As you scale up, you may not be fully available to manage your various videos, interactions and responses. You may need a Virtual Administrator to carry out these tasks on your behalf. This way, you can increase your reach and engagement with your audience.

- Outsource optimization of your Channel – SEO optimization, content optimization, video optimization and all other activities geared towards boosting audience reach and experience can be outsourced. Train and empower your Virtual Administrator to hire and manage Virtual Assistants for each or a collection of these tasks.

- Outsource your content creation – As the scale increases and probably, as your need to relax and retiremennt comes knocking, you may need to hire content creators to help you out. You can hire not only ghostwriters, copywriters, but also those who can do voice-overs and even create an entire video on your behalf. This is possible.

- Outsource marketing of your channel – You can outsource marketing of your channel to a local marketing agency.
- Automate monetization of your channel – There is a limit as to how much income you can derive going it alone or using human effort alone. Thus, you will need the help of others and automation tools. You can have tools to auto-post your Videos or Video clips on all your social media channels. You can engage an Affiliate merchant to sell your YouTube videos on your behalf, you can let advertisers (such as Adsense) market your Channel and even sell your space for ads.

Places to get freelancers

You can hire your Virtual Administrator, Virtual Assistants, Content creators, designers and other such experts on freelance basis. This is by far the best way to go as it is less costly and more effective. Fiverr and Upwork are the most popular one-stop freelancing sites where you can be able to get various types of freelancers to carry out these tasks on affordable terms.

Boosting your YouTube Channel as a source of traffic

YouTube is a great source of traffic. You can use your YouTube Channel to redirect traffic to your other enterprises. Some of these enterprises include;

- Your affiliate products
- Your own Storefront
- Your FBA

Affiliate Products

YouTube is one of the best ways to draw traffic and redirect it to your Affiliate product's page. This is known as Affiliate Marketing. For more information on Affiliate marketing, please refer to an earlier section titled 'Affiliate Marketing'.

Storefront

A storefront is simply a place where customers can visit to buy your products. You can easily create your own online storefront (using ecommerce apps and plugins) whereby you can redirect your YouTube Channel traffic to buy products that you have demonstrated using your YouTube video.

FBA

Fulfillment by Amazon (FBA) simply means letting Amazon fulfill an Order from your customer on your behalf. In essence, it is outsourcing your fulfillment service/function to Amazon. You can create your own private labels and let Amazon fulfill on your behalf.

Private labeling refers to uniquely branding an already existing product so that it appears as a unique product from you. For example, you can buy a plain T-shirt from a supplier and brand it as your name or logo on it. This becomes your private label of the T-shirt.

You can easily redirect traffic from your YouTube Channel to your FBA product page so that your potential customers can buy the product that you have demonstrated using your YouTube video.

CONCLUSION

Thank you for acquiring and reading this book!

This book provides practical hands-on information on how to build a Youtube channel audience and make passive income. It walks you through each and every step to ensure that you succeed.

I hope this book has not only inspired you to become a videopreneur but has also enabled you to earn passive income off your Youtube channel. It is also my sincere hope that, by becoming inspired and successful, you have been able to share information about this guide with others so that they too get inspired and successful. This way, you help build a society of successful entrepreneurs that provide solutions to global challenges.

Again, thank you for acquiring and reading this book.

Good luck!

Printed in Great Britain
by Amazon